The Voters Decision Making Toolkit
for the 2015 Nigerian General Election

First published in Great Britain 2015 by

The Self Publishing Site Ltd

Honiton, Devon

Tel: 01404 841523

Email: info@theselfpublishingsite.co.uk

ISBN: 978-1508926566

Typeset by Randesign UK

Book Design by the Self Publishing Site Ltd

The toolkit is a project in collaboration with the:

Sustainable Development Initiatives in Action CIC (SDIAcic)

Croydon, Surrey. CR0 2XU E: info@sdiacic.com T: +44800 5999 423

CONTENTS

Foreword   4

Acknowledgement   5

Introduction   6

Who is the Toolkit for and its benefits   8

How to use the Toolkit   9

Voters Decides – Political Parties   11

Voters Decides – Candidates:

- Presidential Candidates   19
- Governorship Candidates   23
- Senatorial Candidates   27
- House of Reps Candidates   31
- State House of Assembly Candidates   35
- Blank Copy of Candidates Qualities &
  Characteristics Analysis Table   39

Voting process on the Election Day – Accreditation & Voting   43

Political Parties code of conduct 2013:
Election Day & Post Election Issues   44

About the Author   46

References   47

FOREWORD

I will recommend this toolkit for anybody who intends to fulfil their democratic duty by voting for the right candidate.

By using the criteria set out in the toolkit, you can judge the parties manifestos, assess candidates for all the political positions and assess the suitability of the candidate for the position they are applying for.

This will help the electorate decide whether the candidate qualifies for the position they are applying for.

Councillor Adedamola Aminu

Mayor of Lambeth

London

United Kingdom

11 March 2015

ACKNOWLEDGEMENTS

Many people have contributed to the development of this toolkit. Thank you to all those who provided additional information and ideas including most of the political party leaders that responded to our calls. In particular, my family, the Mayor of Lambeth – Councillor Adedamola Aminu, Mr Amos Adejimi and Mr Ikenna Obianwu.

Elections provide a vital means of safeguarding human rights, exercising choice and expressing opinions. Research suggests that the outcomes for the voters are more positive if they have had the opportunity to make an informed decision about the election. An opportunity to recognise that the decision is theirs and to acknowledge responsibility for their decision.

When we vote in an election, we vote for a candidate to represent our constituency. Each candidate will fight the election on a manifesto. Deciding which candidate to vote into office is simply a matter of party affiliation for many people. Others, however, cast their votes based on specific characteristics they look for in their candidate of choice.

When you take a moment to reflect on yourself and the community you live in and on the country as a whole, you will be able to decide who to vote for in your election based on:

- Issues that motivate you or concern you, or

- Improvements you would like to see in your local area or country as a whole.

The aim of the toolkit is to support Nigerians in exploring all of their options in relation to the election decision. The toolkit encourages the voter to consider the possible short, medium and long-term implications of their options, in order to reach an informed personal decision and to vote wisely.

There are approximately 250 ethnic groups and tribes in Nigeria and each group has its own language. The English language is used to establish uniformity, between and within this diverse cultural mix. The three main indigenous languages spoken by the three predominant ethnic groups are Yorubas in the West, Hausa-Fulani in the North and the Igbos in the East.

We are not partisan nor selective. We have contacted **all** the 28 registered political parties for information and permission to use their logo and candidate image for this task. We have included information on the **voting process and political parties code of conduct issued by INEC in 2013 on Election Day & Post Election issues**, information about **parties** running in the election and their **candidates**.

In addition to the toolkit, we would like to remind you to be prudent in exercising your voter's rights. Many underprivileged Nigerians are vulnerable to pressure and coercion during the election period. They need support to help them make the right voter's choice based on their own needs and desires in relation to the election. Elections really are a great time to influence the decision makers. During this time, the aspiring candidates are more willing to talk to you, and you have a unique opportunity to influence both their immediate quick win promises and longer term plans.

This is a new initiative, feedback from the toolkit users can also then be used as a way of holding the government to account after the election. Mail your feedback to - info@sdiacic.com.

Wishing us all the best in the forthcoming elections.

Thank you.

Everyone plays a role in making the election process free and fair. The right to vote in an election is the heartbeat of every democracy. The act of placing a vote is a momentous and empowering experience. This toolkit is aimed at all Nigerians and it is an arm of voter education:

- Political parties and their aspirants – use it to reassure the electorate of their promises and demonstrate a commitment to actualising those promises. It can be used to increase engagement and support the electorate in their decision making and holding the government accountable after the election. Most political parties participate.

- Voter – use it to increase knowledge about effective decision making, to score prioritised key issues, to be proactive in identifying and making your own choices, to discover personal power in voting rights.

- Youths – to reassure youth that their involvement counts, to encourage political engagement and give confidence to the youth who may not be interested in participating in the election as they do not feel that their vote will make a difference.

- Illiterates – we challenge those of us that are literate to support our household and the illiterate people in our community at large as much as possible, by interpreting the toolkit in local language, provides best description of the political party's key issues and their candidate qualities and character. We should support each other to vote for the best candidates.

To optimise the benefits of the toolkit, we urge the users to take the following steps:

1. Political Party's Choice

   1.1. Check the manifesto of each political party and tick the box accord ingly.

   1.2. Each box ticked is equivalent to one point.

   1.3. Add all the points for each political party and insert the sum in the total column.

   1.4. Rank these totals in the priority column, from the highest total to the lowest.

   1.5. Identify the party that scored the highest points in the priority column.

2. Candidate's Choice

   1.1. Based on your knowledge and findings about the candidate, tick the box which most accurately describes their qualities and character.

   1.2. Each box ticked is equivalent to one point.

   1.3. Add all the points for each candidate and insert the sum in the total column.

   1.4. Rank these totals in the priority column, from the highest total to the lowest.

   1.5. Identify the candidate that scored the highest points in the priority column.

Based on the outcome of your personal assessment, you may decide to cast your vote for the highest scoring party or candidate in the priority column.

Note

- We implore the voters to look at the details of the political party key issues identified in the party manifestos. This will serve at least three purposes:

  o To enhance your knowledge of the issues.

  o To understand the broadness of each selected issue and its policy.

  o To familiarise yourself with each party's policy on that particular issue and vote appropriately.

- Where two or more parties/candidates have equally scored the highest points, decide on whom to select by considering additional qualities and characteristics as you may see fit.

- Every Vote Counts – The candidate with the largest amount of votes is the winner!

On Election Day, as voters, you must take a leap. This exercise may help to see a little more clearly where we might land.

VOTER'S DECIDES – Political Parties Choice

Below are the summary of the few political party's manifestos that are available. Voters should liaise with the political party leaders to get their party manifesto or derived the party key issues from their campaign at various platforms.

KEY TO POLITICAL PARTIES MANIFESTOS

Key	Meaning
Community	Devolution of Power
Corruption	War against corruption and national orientation
Economy	Economy
Education	Education
Employment	Labour employment and wages
Environment	Environmental obligations
Food	Agriculture & food security
Foreign Policy	Foreign policy & international relations
Health	Health
Housing	Housing
Industrialisation	Rapid industrial growth
Infrastructure	Rebuilding and expanding basic infrastructure
Justice	Human rights
Power	Power supply and Energy
Science & Technology	Science & Technology
Security	Security & Defence
Transport	Integrated transport network
Water	Water supply
Welfare & Social Benefits	Welfare & Social Benefits

Logo	Party Name	ACRO-NYM	Com-munity	Cor-ruption	Econ-omy	Educ-ation	Emplo-yment
	Accord	A					
	Action Alliance	AA					
	Advanced Congress of Democrats	ACD					
	Congress PArty of Nigeria	ACPN					
	Alliance for Democracy	AD					
	African Democratic Congress	ADC					
	African Peoples Alliance	APA					
	All Progressives Congress	APC					
	All Progressives Grand Alliance	APGA					
	Citizens Popular Party	CPP					
	Democratic Peoples Party	DPP					
	Fresh Democratic Party	FRESH					
	Hope Democratic Party	HDP					
	Independent Democrats	IP					
	Kowa Party	KP					
	Labour Party	LP					
	Mega Progressive Peoples Party	MPPP					
	National Consience Party	NCP					

Logo	Party Name	ACRO-NYM	Com-munity	Cor-ruption	Econ-omy	Educ-ation	Emplo-yment
	New Nigeria Peo-ples Party	NNPP					
	People for Demo-cratic Change	PDC					
	Peoples Democratic Movement	PDM					
	Peoples Democratic Party	PDP					
	Progressive Peoples Alliance	PPA					
	Peoples Party of Nigeria	PPN					
	Social Democratic Party	SDP					
	United Democratic Party	UDP					
	Unity Party of Nigeria	UPN					
	United Progressive Party	UPP					

ACRO-NYM	Envi-ron-ment	Food / Agricul-ture	Foreign / Int Policy	Health	Housing	Indus-trialisa-tion	Infra-struc-ture	Justice
A								
AA								
ACD								
ACPN								
AD								
ADC								
APA								
APC								
APGA								
CPP								
DPP								
FRESH								
HDP								
IP								
KP								
LP								
MPPP								
NCP								
NNPP								
PDC								
PDM								
PDP								
PPA								
PPN								
SDP								
UDP								
UPN								
UPP								

VOTER'S DECIDES – POLITICAL PARTIES CHOICE

ACRO-NYM	Power / Elec-tricty	Food / Agricul-ture	Security / De-fence	Trans-porta-tion	Water / Sanita-tion	Welfare & Social Benefits	Total	Priority
A								
AA								
ACD								
ACPN								
AD								
ADC								
APA								
APC								
APGA								
CPP								
DPP								
FRESH								
HDP								
IP								
KP								
LP								
MPPP								
NCP								
NNPP								
PDC								
PDM								
PDP								
PPA								
PPN								
SDP								
UDP								
UPN								
UPP								

On general terms, you may vote based on what the party denotes and its notion as it may be:

Denote	Notion
Vision	Has a plan for everyone
Tomorrow	Wants to shape the future
Change	Wants progress for Nigeria
Transformation	Wants to make a difference
Progress	Will move Nigeria forward

VOTER'S DECIDES – Candidate Choice

The simplest way to evaluate a candidate's character, is to simply ask them how they intend to actualise their promises and intended programmes. This puts the voter in a better position to evaluate the candidate's theoretical position. The candidate has to have the necessary skills to follow through on his/her promises and translate his/her position into policy. Focusing more on the character of candidates may get the voter's closer to understanding how the candidate would operate in the office. According to our research, the qualities or characteristics that good political leaders should possess are as indicated in the table below. What do you see in your candidates?

KEY	MEANING
Ambitious in Policy	Able to contribute to the success of the nation and make life better for people
Charismatic /Build Consensus	Likeable by people
Clear Vision / Foresight	Be clear as to who he/she is and what is most important to him/her
Communicate Effectively	Very good at public speaking, making speeches and possibly oratory
Courageous	Not afraid to take risks or make mistakes and believe in him/herself
Empowering	Make his/her associates feel emboldened and powerful, not diminished and powerless
Focus	Have a strong stated mission to lead
Good & Indifferent	Know how to use the system to achieve results
Honest / Trustworthy	Honest and trusted by those under him/her
Innovative	Innovative in solving critical problems and improve people thinking
Integrity	Respected and worth listening to, be honest and meet his/her commitment
Intelligent / Knowledgeable / Resourcefulness	Able to forge agreement on policy or political goals, take defeat in stride, quick to learn from them and move forward.
Judgment / Just	Includes when to keep things secret and when to go public
Loyal	Not forget where he/she is from and have an abiding faith in the decency, intelligence and patriotism of the voters
Management Ability	Able to make decision, lead subordinate, admit mistakes and learn from them
Moral authority	To lead by moral authority and represents all that is best in his/her countrymen
Passionate	Have vision for the future and seeks to make it come true.
Patriotism	Love of and devotion to Nigeria with vigorous support for the hopes, dreams, and interests of ordinary citizens
Persuasiveness / Image / good speech	Able to deliver a good speech and read public opinion
Political Skill	Must be able to read the political landscape he/she may face when they get to office'
Principled / Firm	Having strong ideals
Responsible / Decent	Take responsibility for the decision he/she make - do not pass the buck or blame other people
Temperament	Handle erratic and unpredictable pressures of the office and real uncertainty
Vitality /Strong / Active /Energy	Healthy

Photograph	Name of Candidate	Qualification	Ambitious in Policy	Charismatic / Build Consensus	Clear Vision / Foresight	Communicate Effectively
	jci sen. tunde anifowose-kelani					
	rafiu salau					
	alh. ganiyu o. galadima					
	dr. mani ibrahim ahmad					
	ayeni musa adebayo					
	muhammadu buhari					
	chief sam eke					
	high chief ambrose n. albert owuru					
	comfort oluremi sonaiya					
	chief martin onovo					
	goodluck ebele jonathan					
	allagoa kelvin chinedu					
	godson mgbodile ohaenyem okoye					
	chief (dr.) chekwas okorie					

Name of Candidate	Coura-geous	Em-power-ing	Focus	Good & Indif-ferent	Honest / Trust-worthy	Innova-tive	Integ-rity
jci sen. tunde anifow-ose-kelani							
rafiu salau							
alh. ganiyu o. galadima							
dr. mani ibrahim ahmad							
ayeni musa adebayo							
muhammadu buhari							
chief sam eke							
high chief ambrose n. albert owuru							
comfort oluremi sonaiya							
chief martin onovo							
goodluck ebele jona-than							
allagoa kelvin chinedu							
godson mgbodile ohae-nyem okoye							
chief (dr.) chekwas okorie							

PRESIDENTIAL CANDIDATES

Name of Candidate	Intelligent / Resourcefullness	Judgment	Loyal	Management Ability	Moral Authority	Passionate	Patriotism
jci sen. tunde anifow-ose-kelani							
rafiu salau							
alh. ganiyu o. galadima							
dr. mani ibrahim ahmad							
ayeni musa adebayo							
muhammadu buhari							
chief sam eke							
high chief ambrose n. albert owuru							
comfort oluremi sonaiya							
chief martin onovo							
goodluck ebele jona-than							
allagoa kelvin chinedu							
godson mgbodile ohae-nyem okoye							
chief (dr.) chekwas okorie							

PRESIDENTIAL CANDIDATES

Name of Candidate	Persausiveness / Image / Good speech	Political Skill	Principled / Firm	Responsible / Decent	Temperament	Vitality / Strong / Active	Total	Priority
jci sen. tunde anifow-ose-kelani								
rafiu salau								
alh. ganiyu o. galadima								
dr. mani ibrahim ahmad								
ayeni musa adebayo								
muhammadu buhari								
chief sam eke								
high chief ambrose n. albert owuru								
comfort oluremi sonaiya								
chief martin onovo								
goodluck ebele jona-than								
allagoa kelvin chinedu								
godson mgbodile ohae-nyem okoye								
chief (dr.) chekwas okorie								

GOVERNORSHIP CANDIDATES

Name of Candidate	Quali-fication	Ambi-tious in Policy	Char-asmatic / Build Con-sensus	Clear Vision / Fore-sight	Com-mu-nicate Effec-tively	Coura-geous	Em-power-ing

GOVERNORSHIP CANDIDATES

Name of Candidate	Focus	Good & Indif-ferent	Honest / Trust-worthy	Inno-vative	Integ-rity	Nt / Re-source-fullness	Judge-ment / Just

GOVERNORSHIP CANDIDATES

Name of Candidate	Loyal	Man-age-ment Ability	Moral Au-thority	Pas-sionate	Patriot-ism	Iveness / Image / Good	Poil-itical Skill

GOVERNORSHIP CANDIDATES

Name of Candidate	Princi-pled / Firm	Respon-sible / Decent	Temper-ament	Vitality / Strong / Active	Total	Priority

Name of Candidate	Quali-fication	Ambi-tious in Policy	Char-asmatic / Build Con-sensus	Clear Vision / Fore-sight	Com-mu-nicate Effec-tively	Coura-geous	Em-power-ing

SENATORIAL CANDIDATES

Name of Candidate	Focus	Good & Indif-ferent	Honest / Trust-worthy	Inno-vative	Integ-rity	Nt / Re-source-fullness	Judge-ment / Just

SENATORIAL CANDIDATES

Name of Candidate	Loyal	Man-age-ment Ability	Moral Au-thority	Pas-sionate	Patriot-ism	Iveness / Image / Good	Poil-itical Skill

SENATORIAL CANDIDATES

Name of Candidate	Princi-pled / Firm	Respon-sible / Decent	Temper-ament	Vitality / Strong / Active	Total	Priority

Name of Candidate	Qualification	Ambitious in Policy	Charasmatic / Build Consensus	Clear Vision / Foresight	Communicate Effectively	Courageous	Empowering

HOUSE OF REPS CANDIDATES

Name of Candidate	Focus	Good & Indifferent	Honest / Trustworthy	Innovative	Integrity	Nt / Resourcefullness	Judgement / Just

HOUSE OF REPS CANDIDATES

Name of Candidate	Loyal	Man-age-ment Ability	Moral Au-thority	Pas-sionate	Patriot-ism	Iveness / Image / Good	Poil-itical Skill

HOUSE OF REPS CANDIDATES

Name of Candidate	Princi-pled / Firm	Respon-sible / Decent	Temper-ament	Vitality / Strong / Active	Total	Priority

STATE HOUSE OF ASSEMBLY CANDIDATES

Name of Candidate	Quali-fication	Ambi-tious in Policy	Char-asmatic / Build Con-sensus	Clear Vision / Fore-sight	Com-mu-nicate Effec-tively	Coura-geous	Em-power-ing

STATE HOUSE OF ASSEMBLY CANDIDATES

Name of Candidate	Focus	Good & Indifferent	Honest / Trustworthy	Innovative	Integrity	Nt / Resourcefullness	Judgement / Just

STATE HOUSE OF ASSEMBLY CANDIDATES

Name of Candidate	Loyal	Man-age-ment Ability	Moral Au-thority	Pas-sionate	Patriot-ism	Iveness / Image / Good	Poil-itical Skill

STATE HOUSE OF ASSEMBLY CANDIDATES

Name of Candidate	Princi-pled / Firm	Respon-sible / Decent	Temper-ament	Vitality / Strong / Active	Total	Priority

Name of Candidate	Quali-fication	Ambi-tious in Policy	Char-asmatic / Build Con-sensus	Clear Vision / Fore-sight	Com-mu-nicate Effec-tively	Coura-geous	Em-power-ing

Name of Candidate	Focus	Good & Indifferent	Honest / Trustworthy	Innovative	Integrity	Nt / Resourcefullness	Judgement / Just

Name of Candidate	Loyal	Man-age-ment Ability	Moral Au-thority	Pas-sionate	Patriot-ism	Iveness / Image / Good	Poil-itical Skill

Name of Candidate	Princi-pled / Firm	Respon-sible / Decent	Temper-ament	Vitality / Strong / Active	Total	Priority

STAGE 1: ACCREDITATION

Step 1: Go to the Polling Unit you were registered with your voter registration card and join the queue.

Step 2: Present your Voter registration card to the INEC official and ensure that your name is in the register.

Step 3: Your finger would be marked with ink to show that you have been accredited.

STAGE 2: VOTING

Step 1: Join the queue with the intention of casting your vote.

Step 2: When it gets to your turn, ensure your name is ticked in the voter register.

Step 3: You would be given a ballot paper listing out the political parties.

Step 4: Enter the booth and select your preferred candidate.

Step 5: Place your ballot paper in the ballot box.

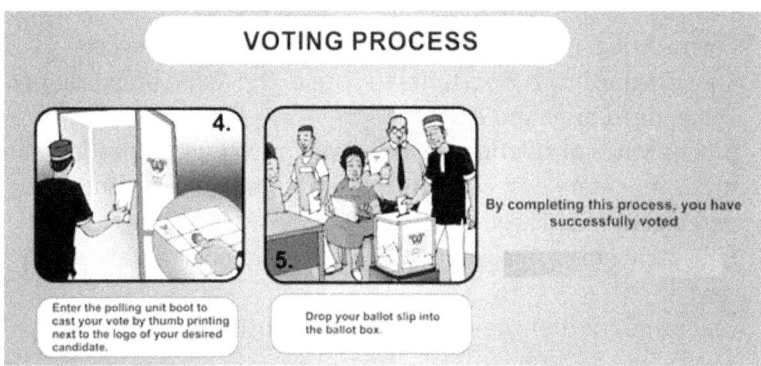

ELECTION DAY ISSUES

1. Political parties, their candidates and agents shall respect the law restricting access of unauthorized persons to polling stations, collation centre's, and discourage undue interference with the voting process.
2. Every party shall instruct its members and supporters that no weapons or any object that can be used to cause injury shall be brought to the polling station, and that no party attire; colours, symbols, emblems or other insignia shall be worn to a polling station on Election Day.
3. Political parties shall recognize and acknowledge the rights of accredited observers and monitors at polling stations for the purpose of observing the conduct of elections and shall grant full lawful access to party activities to such observers.
4. All political parties and their candidates shall ensure that their Polling Agents and officials are sufficiently trained to monitor the voting exercise to ensure free and fair elections.
5. Political parties, their candidates and members shall cooperate fully with law enforcement agents to ensure the safety and security of election materials, election officials, party agents, and the electorates on Election Day.
6. Political parties shall refrain from fraudulently procuring results and votes by invasion and forcible occupation of polling and collation Centre, the manipulation of ballot boxes, result sheets or by any other unlawful means.
7. Political parties and their agents shall not engage in any of the following corrupt practices:
    a. Forcible occupation or invasion of a polling station, collation Centre or INEC office;
    b. Destroy any electoral material or INEC property;
    c. Encouraging any supporter(s) to cast more than one vote;
    d. Encouraging any supporter(s) to vote in the name of another person, living, dead or fictitious;
    e. Buying votes or offering any bribe, gift, reward, gratification or any other monetary or materials consideration of allurement to voters and electoral officials;
    f. Canvassing for votes within the vicinity of a polling station on polling day;
    g. Any other form of cheating or any act considered to be a malpractice

under the electoral laws and regulations.

h. Political parties, their candidates and their agents shall not obstruct, harass or intimidate journalists in the course of their duties.

8. All political parties, their candidates and their agents' party members and supporters shall accept the official election results as certified by INEC as free and fair, or challenge the results in court.

POST ELECTION ISSUES

1. Political parties shall not intimidate, harass or cajole any polling agent of a political party to sign election result, if in the judgment of such an agent the election in the polling station was not free and fair.

2. No political party, their candidates or agents shall procure election results fraudulently or manipulate collation sheets, ballot boxes or cause to be published or displayed by the electronic and print media such unofficial or fraudulent results, except those published or announced by INEC.

3. Political parties and their candidates shall endeavor to send congratulatory messages to their opponents who are announced as duly elected.

4. All political parties and their candidates shall refrain from the use of violent or extra judicial means in expressing their non-acceptance of election results.

5. Political parties and their candidates shall ensure strict adherence to provisions of the law in seeking redress against perceived electoral irregularities.

This resource was written by: Maroof Akintunde Adeoye a patriotic Nigerian diaspora living in the United Kingdom with major interest in the actualisation of sustainable development in Nigeria. Mr Adeoye holds a Master of Business Administration (MBA) in the UK in 1993 and is a graduate of the Institute of Chartered Accountant in England and Wales (ICAEW) with Diploma in Charity Accounting (DChA). Mr Adeoye was a member of the Charity and Voluntary Sector Special Interest Group and a graduate of the Chartered Institute of Marketing (CIM) in 1986 with protracted experience in working with and raising funds for Civil Society Organisations. Mr Adeoye is also a fellow of the Association of Charity Independent Examiners (FCIE), a full member of the Institute of Fundraising (MInstF), a member of the Nigerian Institute of Management (MNIM) chartered, a qualified trainer with Preparing to Teach in the Lifelong Learning Sector (PTLLS) and Prince2 project management foundation qualified. Mr Adeoye has participated in so many management and developmental programmes, including Cambridge University Judge Business School Africa Business Network `Breaking Myths About Success' and was a UK delegate for the 10th World Islamic Economic Forum in Dubai. Mr Adeoye is a successful Social Entrepreneur, a director at Sustainable Development Initiatives in Action CIC (SDIAcic) UK.

SDIAcic is a non-partisan, civil society organisation, structured as a community interest company registered in the United Kingdom. The SDIAcic objective is to carry on activities which benefit the community and, in particular, (without limitation) to social progress which recognises the needs of everyone; effective protection of the environment; prudent use of natural resources; maintenance of high and stable levels of economic growth and employment. A key SDIAcic aim is to support the bolstering of human capital, improvement of infrastructure, social, economic and political rights that will ultimately enhance basic standards of living.

REFERENCES

- Independent National Electoral Commission (INEC)
- Best Practice Toolkit: Pregnancy decision-making support for teenagers Education for Choice
- Module 3 Decision-Making Tools – Basic Tools for Process Im provement, Balanced Scorecard Institute
- UK Parliament – Elections and voting – www.parliament.uk
- John Dickerson is Slate's chief political correspondent, Article – How To Measure for a President 2012
- The Center On Congress at Indiana University – What Makes A Good Politician?
- Beliefnet.com – Top 5 Qualities of Good Political Leaders

www.ingramcontent.com/pod-product-compliance
Lightning Source LLC
Chambersburg PA
CBHW071011180526
45168CB00003B/1379